Doodle A

Rabbits & Hares

Annette Rand

www.doodleartist.co.uk

Contents

2 copies of each picture

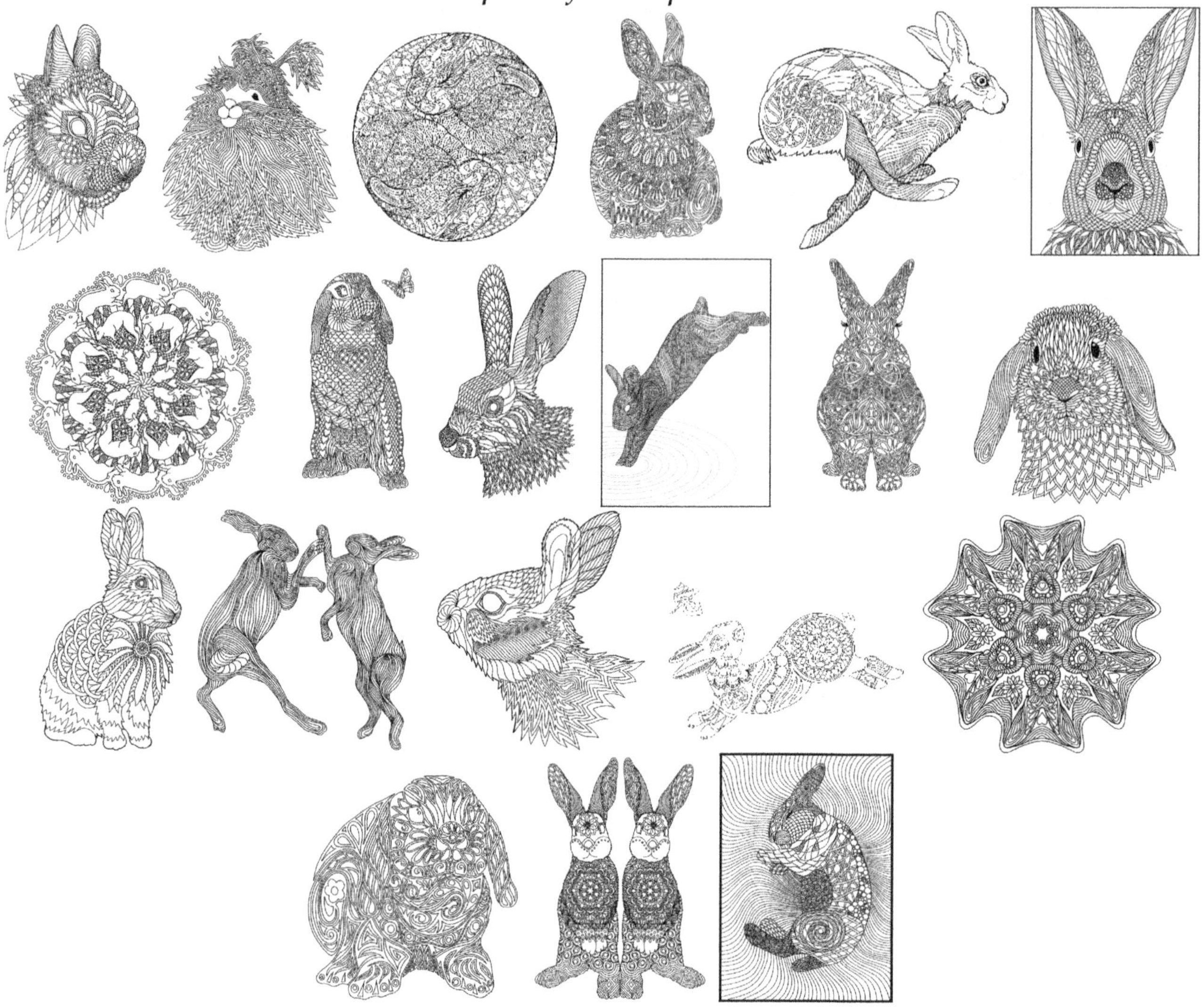

ISBN-13: 978-1519452634

ISBN-10: 1519452632

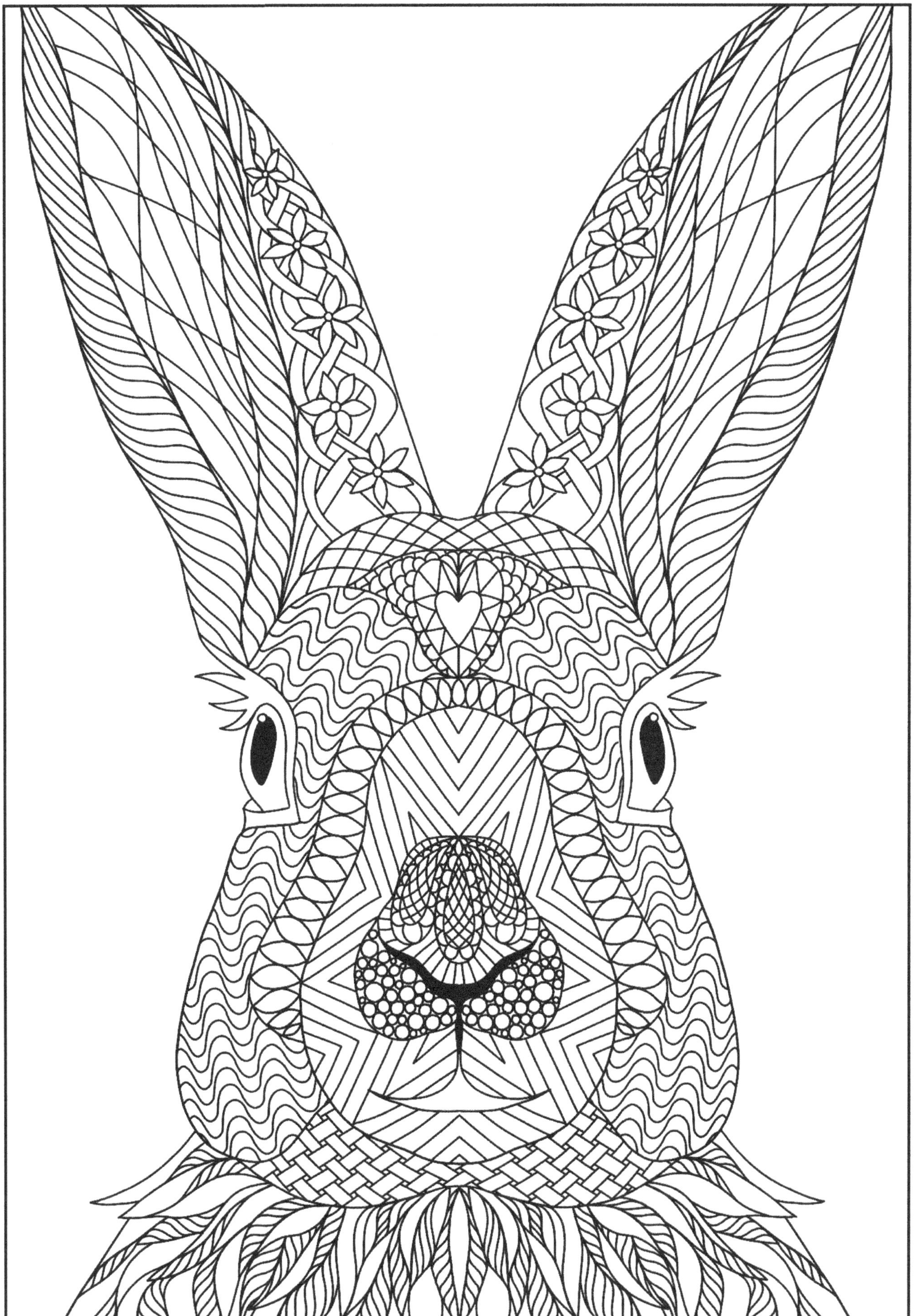

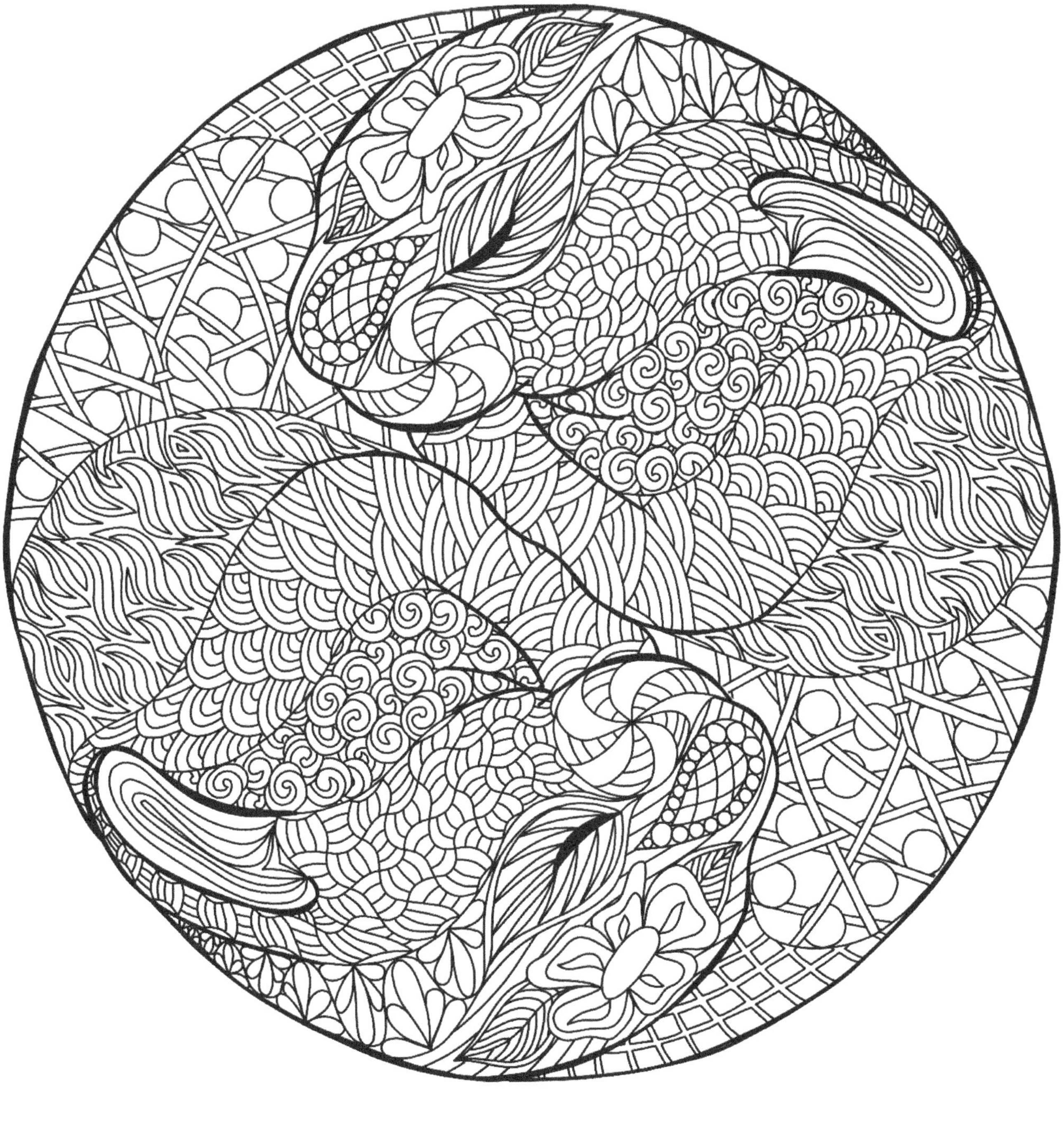

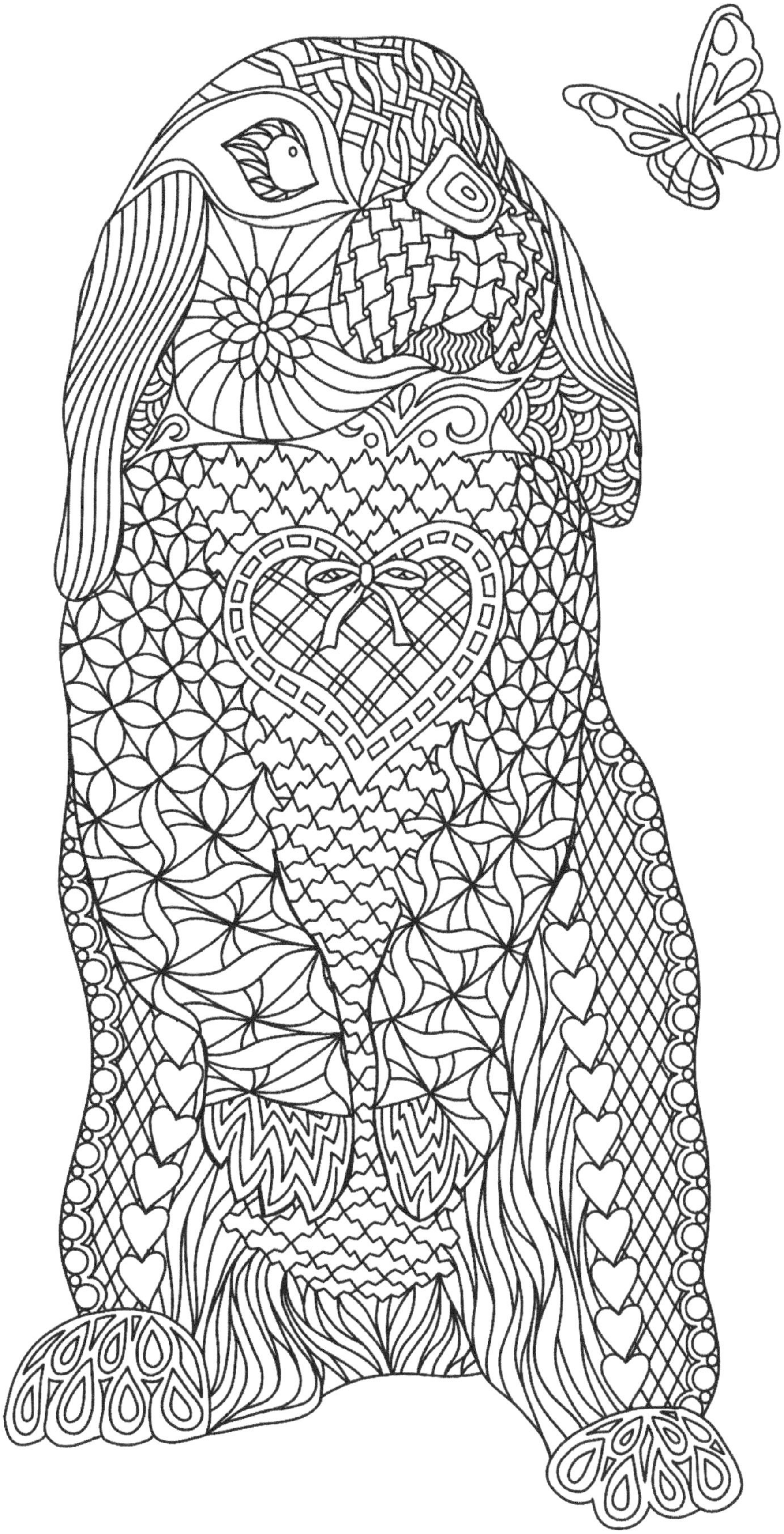

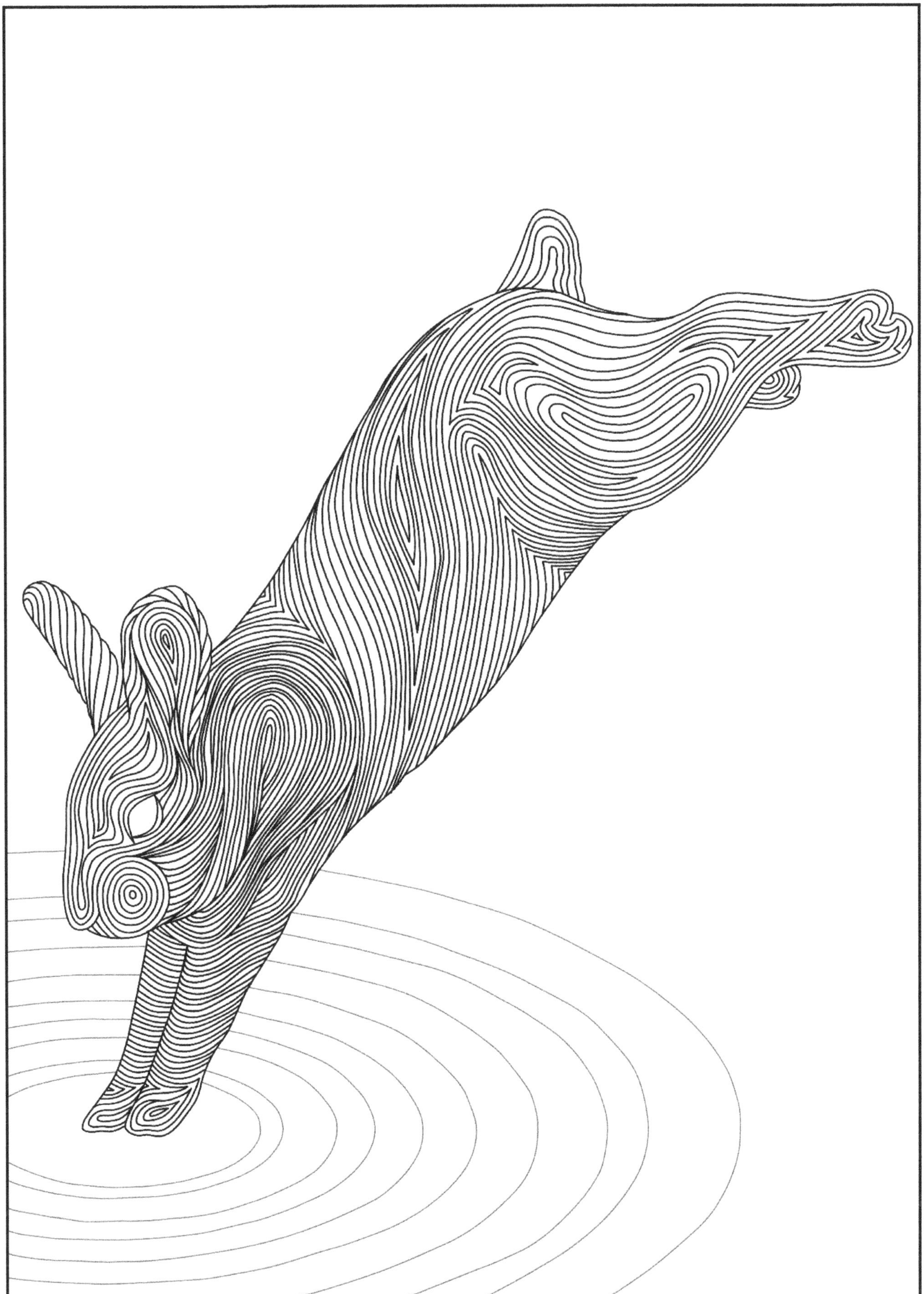

Made in the USA
Monee, IL
26 March 2021

63911916R00046